This delightful book is the latest in the series of Ladybird books which have been specially planned to help grown-ups with the world about them.

As in the other books in this series, the large clear script, the careful choice of words, the frequent repetition and the thoughtful matching of text with pictures all enable grown-ups to think they have taught themselves to cope. The subject of the book will greatly appeal to grown-ups.

Series 999

THE LADYBIRD
BOOKS FOR GROWN–UPS SERIES

THE
MEETING

by

J.A. HAZELEY, N.S.F.W. and J.P. MORRIS, O.M.G.

(Authors of 'King Dinosaur The Christmas Pirate Wizard')

Publishers: Ladybird Books Ltd., Loughborough
Printed in England. If wet, Italy.

People at work spend a lot of the day in meetings.

Meetings are important because they give everyone a chance to talk about work.

Which is easier than doing it.

Adam looks at his watch.

Every second that ticks away is time he has spent discussing the company's display stand at the Frankfurt Bathroom Expo.

Adam's life is being consumed, piece by tiny piece, while he pretends to care about taps.

At a meeting, everyone has a chance to have their say.

Most of the people at this meeting have nothing to say, but they say something anyway.

That way the meeting has not been a waste of everyone's time.

You can tell a lot about a meeting from the refreshments.

If there is a bowl of fruit on the table, the meeting is very serious, and has probably been organised by an unhappy person.

If there are biscuits, it is a happy meeting — especially if there are those Lemon Puffs that do not seem to be in the shops any more.

Try not to think about how long they must have been in the cupboard.

Katy gets the 6.15 train every Monday morning so she does not miss the eight o'clock team meeting.

It is very early and the man next to her has been snoring in the crook of her neck since Winnersh Triangle, but at least she gets a seat.

Katy checks her newspaper in case there are any vacanies for a freelance hermit.

Rudd attends meetings remotely from his home office.

He has three telephones, two Swiss desk intercoms, a fax machine and a wall—mounted theremin.

Sometimes, nobody speaks to him for days.

The facilitator has used the white-board to illustrate The Hexagon Of Unexpectedness.

Shireen thinks the facilitator looks very pleased with himself.

But people who say "pacifically" when they mean "specifically" tend to be very easily pleased.

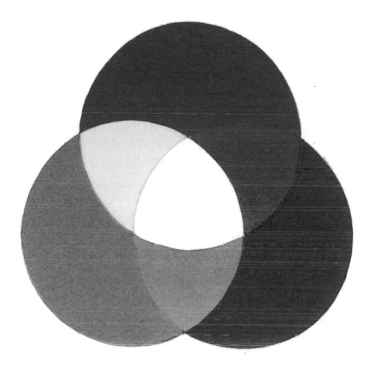

Mr Beverley is reading out a 60-page document entitled "The Paperless Office".

Yesterday Mr Beverley emailed the document to everyone and told them to read it before the meeting, which they all did.

Just in case, he hands everyone a printed copy.

Mr Beverley finds the sound of the shredder relaxing.

Jethro recently learned the word "upskilling", and is now using it three or four times per meeting.

"Jethro is really offcheesing me," thinks Nathan.

There are two break—out zones in the offices of this human rights' charity in Bristol. One has a slide in it — the other has a fully licensed bar.

"Which one shall we meet in?" Jess asks her team.

They have not chosen the one with the slide in it.

Nobody ever does.

A meeting will stay on–topic if it has an agenda.

A common agenda might start with "Why will my computer not work with the screen in this room?" then move on to "Is there another lead?" and "Is there another computer?" and finally "Is there another room?"

Then giving up and sandwiches.

A SMALL DIGITAL COMPUTER
DESIGNED FOR THE BUSINESSMAN

A LARGE COMPUTER INSTALLATION

Nicola is having a meeting to draw up a new contract defining her role as a knowledge transfer partnership provider who drives local footprint cost savings as laid out in the forward sustainable resource outlay architecture process.

Nicola cannot see the word "teaching" in her contract, but she has so little time to do that these days, what with all the meetings.

These important people are discussing work-place diversity.

Rowland and Dan are having an informal chat before going into their pre—meeting about the meeting to discuss the pre—conference plans for this year's conference.

Rowland has had a tooth—ache for six months, but has not had the time to meet the dentist.

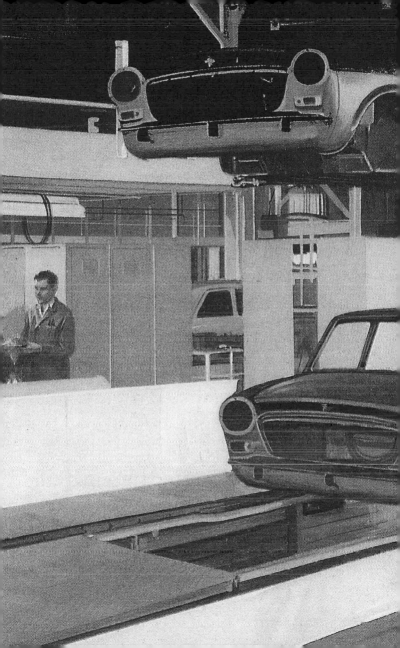

Brian and Mandy are away from the office on a course.

Yesterday they played basketball without a ball until they understood inclusivity. Today they are optimising alternative mindpaths by turning some old dust sheets into a ghost.

The course is entitled "Identifying Monetizing Opportunities" and costs £1,400 per person.

A conference call can take the place of a meeting.

So far Grant's project team have only managed to say three things without talking over the top of each other — "Hello", "Sorry" and "Shall we have a proper meeting?"

Anna asked her P.A. to book somewhere memorable for the company's senior management review.

No—one can get on to the Wi—Fi network, but the torpedo button is proving very popular.

Desmond is self-employed. He has booked an all-expenses-claimed away-day for himself at an hotel in Corby.

There were three main sessions: breakfast, lunch and a type of tax-deductible massage.

Vito was busy putting a rival businessman in cement when he had to stop and go to a meeting with Don Carpetti.

"Why are more of my rivals not in cement?" shouts Don Carpetti. "What are you bums doing all day? Waterskiing?"

Vito thinks about explaining, but he does not want to be put in cement.

Zoe has provided a laminated list of her achievements for her annual appraisal.

The list mentions all the laminated A4 notices Zoe has put up around the office. She has also laminated a sign above the laminator about correct use of the laminator.

Her line manager asks Zoe if she has a weakness for the laminator.

Zoe is too high on laminator fumes to care.

Mr Bideford does not like meetings, so he is going in his cupboard again.

To save time, the committee of The Worshipful Company Of Victorian Time Travellers simply travels back to the beginning of the meeting if nothing useful is decided, and starts again.

They have been trapped in this room for eleven million years.

An earlier accident on the M62 has made Jacqui very late for her wash—up meeting, so she is conference calling from the car.

She cannot concentrate on the road or the call, and it will be some time before she realises she is going the wrong way.

The earlier accident on the M62 was caused by someone a lot like Jacqui.